Smoothies For The Absolute Beginner

Franklin F. Brewer

Introduction

Welcome to this book, a delightful and nutritious journey into the world of blended goodness. If you're new to the smoothie scene, you're in for a treat! This guide is designed to introduce you to the wonderful world of smoothies and help you create delicious, vibrant, and healthy blends right in your kitchen.

Smoothies have gained popularity for good reason – they are not only incredibly delicious but also packed with essential nutrients, vitamins, and minerals. Whether you're looking to kickstart your day with a nutritious breakfast or satisfy your sweet tooth with a guilt-free treat, smoothies offer a wide range of options to suit your tastes and dietary preferences.

In this guide, we'll explore a variety of smoothie recipes in different colors and flavors. Each chapter will take you on a flavorful journey, showcasing the abundant possibilities that smoothies offer. From refreshing green blends to luscious purple creations, you'll discover a rainbow of choices to tantalize your taste buds.

The first chapter, "Green Smoothies," is a great starting point for beginners. Packed with leafy greens, fruits, and other wholesome ingredients, green smoothies are a fantastic way to boost your energy levels and incorporate more greens into your diet. These blends are not only nutritious but also incredibly refreshing, making them perfect for a morning pick-me-up or a post-workout treat.

If you're in the mood for something sunny and bright, the "Yellow Smoothies" chapter is sure to delight. Bursting with vibrant fruits like mangoes, pineapples, and bananas, these smoothies will transport you to a tropical paradise with every sip. The combination of sweet and tangy flavors will leave you feeling refreshed and energized.

In contrast, the "White Smoothies" chapter offers a unique twist, featuring blends that are rich, creamy, and dairy-free. These smoothies are perfect for those with lactose sensitivities or anyone looking for a lighter, non-dairy option. From coconut-based delights to nutty concoctions, you'll discover a wide array of flavors to satisfy your taste buds.

The "Rainbow Smoothie" chapter is a true celebration of colors and flavors, combining a variety of fruits and vegetables to create visually stunning blends. These smoothies are not only a feast for the eyes but also a nutrient-packed treat for your body. Each color in the rainbow brings its own unique health benefits, making these blends both delicious and nutritious.

If you're craving a bold and intense flavor profile, the "Red Smoothies" chapter is for you. Bursting with the sweetness of berries and cherries, these blends are both delicious and packed with antioxidants. From tangy raspberry blends to indulgent strawberry treats, you'll find a red smoothie to suit your taste.

Finally, the "Purple Smoothies" chapter offers a delightful collection of blends that are as beautiful as they are delicious. With a combination of blueberries, blackberries, and other vibrant ingredients, these smoothies are not only visually appealing but also loaded with antioxidants and health benefits.

In this book, the possibilities are endless, and the journey is delicious. Whether you're a health enthusiast, a culinary explorer, or just looking for a delightful way to improve your nutrition, smoothies are the perfect addition to your daily routine. So, grab your blender and join us on this flavorful adventure!

Contents

GREEN SMOOTHIES...1

Kale Kiwi Apple Smoothie 1

Zucchini Apples Smoothie 2

Dandelion Smoothie 3

Broccoli Apple Smoothie 4

Salad Smoothie 5

Avocado Kale Smoothie 6

Watercress Smoothie 7

Beet Greens Smoothie 8

Broccoli Leeks Cucumber smoothie...9

Cacao Spinach Smoothie 10

Flax Almond Butter Smoothie..11

Apple Kale Smoothie...12

Iceberg Peach Smoothie 13

Kiwi Apple & Leaf Lettuce Smoothie 14

Banana Spinach Raspberry Smoothie 15

Endive Apples Smoothie 16

Spinach Celery Parsley Smoothie..17

Cucumber Spinach Celery Carrot Smoothie 18

Kale Cucumber Lime Apples Smoothie 19

Kiwi Zucchini Smoothie 20

Avocado Kale Smoothie 21

Flax Kiwi Spinach Smoothie..22

Parsley Arugula Cucumber Apples Smoothie.................................23

Celery Cucumber Cabbage Apples Smoothie 24

Kale Banana Apples Smoothie 25

Zucchini Celery Apples Smoothie 26

Leaf Lettuce Apples Spinach Smoothie 27

Zucchini Parsley Smoothie 28

Dandelion Banana Smoothie 29

Leaf Lettuce Parsley Smoothie 30

Chia Apples Spinach Smoothie 31

Grapefruit Kale Watercress Smoothie 32

Collard Greens Parsley and Banana Smoothie 33

Dandelion Apples Smoothie 34

Arugula Celery Apples Smoothie 35

Barley Grass Smoothie 36

Yellow Smoothies 37

Cauliflower Smoothie 37

Mango Pineapple Smoothie 38

Swiss Papaya Smoothie 39

Apple Pineapple Smoothie 40

Kiwi & Cauliflower Smoothie 41

Cantaloupe Mango & Kiwi Smoothie 42

Banana & Mango Smoothie 43

Pineapple, Mango & Spinach Smoothie 44

Peach & Pineapple Smoothie 45

Maracuja Chia Mango Avocado Smoothie 46

Ginger Mango Mint Yellow Pumpkin Smoothie 47

Orange & Mango Smoothie 48

Avocado Mango Smoothie 49

WHITE SMOOTHIES 50

   Coconut Chia Pudding 50

   White Kefir Smoothie.. 51

   Tzataziki Smoothie 52

   Coconut Smoothie.. 53

   Cacao Blackberries Chia Pudding 54

   Coconut Yogurt Smoothie 55

   Coconut Pomegranate Chia Pudding.. 56

Rainbow Smoothie 57

   3 Colors Rainbow Smoothie... 57

RED SMOOTHIES 58

   Carrot Date Smoothie... 58

   Watermelon Apple smoothie 59

   Watermelon Red Grapefruit Smoothie 60

   Strawberry Carrot Smoothie 61

   Apricots & Carrots Smoothie 62

   Strawberries Yogurt Smoothie.. 63

   Red Leaf Lettuce Smoothie 64

   Papaya Diva Smoothie... 65

   Pomegranates & Berries smoothie 66

   Avocado Carrot Smoothie 67

   Red Currants Mellon Smoothie 68

   Blood Orange Smoothie 69

   Papaya Red Spinach Smoothie 70

   Rainbow Smoothie 71

   Frozen Berries Smoothie.. 72

   Superfoods Smoothie Popsicles 73

Pomegranate Watermelon Smoothie 74

Orange Carrot Smoothie 75

Carrot Orange Papaya Smoothie 76

Carrot Date Smoothie 77

Pomegranate Yogurt Smoothie 78

Mango Papaya Mint Smoothie 79

Papaya Carrot Pineapple Smoothie 80

Quatro Lamponi Mirtillo Negress Ribes Smoothie (4 BerriesSmoothie) 81

Berries Kefir Smoothie 82

Red Currants Blueberry Smoothie 83

Cucumber Carrot Date Smoothie 84

Raspberry Sesame Smoothie 85

Raspberry Cucumber Smoothie 86

Blackberry Kefir Smoothie 87

Cantaloupe Raspberry red Currant Smoothie 88

Papaya Cauliflower Smoothie 89

Pumpkin Date Smoothie 90

Pumpkin Kefir Smoothie 91

Cantaloupe Papaya Smoothie 92

PURPLE SMOOTHIES 93

Red Dragon Fruit (Pitaya) Smoothie 93

Blueberry Yogurt & Chard Smoothie 94

Beet Apple Smoothie 95

Blueberry Avocado Smoothie 96

Purple Beet Smoothie 97

Red Grapefruit & Beets Smoothie 98

Blueberry Banana Smoothie 99

Purple Endive & Fig Smoothie 100

Purple Queen Smoothie 101

Black Smoothie 102

Blueberry Kefir & Spinach Smoothie 103

Blackberry Yogurt & Purple Carrots Smoothie 104

Blackberry Banana Smoothie 105

Blueberry & Coconut Smoothie 106

Blueberry, Coconut Flakes & Sesame Seeds Smoothie.......................... 107

Blueberry & Kefir Smoothie 108

Blueberry & Almond Smoothie 109

Blueberry & Oatmeal Smoothie 110

Dragon Fruit & Banana Smoothie 111

Blueberry & Strawberry Smoothie 112

Blueberry, Kefir & Oats Smoothie 113

Raspberry, Oats & Blueberry Smoothie 114

Double Currants Smoothie 115

Blueberry & Dandelion Smoothie 116

Red Currants, Broccoli & Black Currants Smoothie 117

Frozen Berries, Yogurt & Banana Smoothie 118

Blueberry, Kefir, Coconut & Oats Smoothie 119

Blueberry Raspberry & Tahini Smoothie 120

Raspberry, Blueberry & Endive Smoothie.. 121

Banana, Chia & Blueberry Smoothie 122

GREEN SMOOTHIES

Kale Kiwi Apple Smoothie

- 1 cup Kale, chopped

- 2 Apples

- 3 Kiwis

- 1 tablespoon flax seed

- 1 tablespoon royal jelly (optional)

- 1 cup crushed ice

Zucchini Apples Smoothie

- 1/2 cup zucchini

- 2 Apples

- 3/4 avocado

- 1 stalk Celery

- 1 Lemon

- 1 tbsp. Spirulina (optional)

- 1 1/2 cups crushed ice

Dandelion Smoothie

- 1 cup Dandelion greens (optional)

- 1 cup Spinach

- ½ cup tahini

- 1 Red Radish

- 1 tbsp. Chia seeds

- 1 cup lavender tea (optional) or crushed ice

Broccoli Apple Smoothie

- 1 Apple

- 1 cup Broccoli

- 1 tbsp. Cilantro

- 1 Celery stalk

- 1 cup crushed ice

- 1 tbsp. crushed Seaweed (optional)

Salad Smoothie

- 1 cup spinach
- ½ cucumber
- 1/2 small onion
- 2 tablespoons Parsley
- 2 tablespoons lemon juice
- 1 cup crushed ice
- 1 tbsp. olive oil
- ¼ cup Wheatgrass (optional)

Avocado Kale Smoothie

- 1 cup Kale

- ½ Avocado

- 1 cup Cucumber

- 1 Celery Stalk

- 1 tbsp. Chia seeds

- 1 cup chamomile tea

- 1 tbsp. Spirulina (optional)

Watercress Smoothie

- 1 cup Watercress

- ½ cup almond butter

- 2 small cucumbers

- 1 cup coconut milk

- 1 tbsp. Chlorella (optional)

- 1 tbsp. Black cumin– sprinkle on top and garnish with parsley (optional)

Beet Greens Smoothie

- 1 cup Beet Greens

- 2 tbsp. Pumpkin seeds butter

- 1 cup Strawberry

- 1 tbsp. Sesame seeds

- 1 tbsp. Hemp seeds (optional)

- 1 cup chamomile tea

Broccoli Leeks Cucumber smoothie

- 1 cup Broccoli

- 2 tbsp. Cashew butter

- 2 Leeks

- 2 Cucumbers

- 1 Lime

- ½ cup Lettuce

- ½ cup Leaf Lettuce

- 1 tbsp. Matcha (optional)

- 1 cup crushed ice

Cacao Spinach Smoothie

- 2 cups spinach

- 1 cup blueberries, frozen

- 1 tablespoons dark cocoa powder

- ½ cup unsweetened almond milk

- 1/2 cup crushed ice

- 1 tsp raw honey

- 1 tbsp. Matcha powder (optional)

Flax Almond Butter Smoothie

- ½ cup plain yogurt
- 2 tablespoons almond butter
- 2 cups spinach
- 1 banana, frozen
- 3 strawberries
- 1/2 cup crushed ice
- 1 teaspoon flax seed

Apple Kale Smoothie

- 1 cup kale

- ½ cup coconut milk

- 1 tbsp. Maca

- 1 banana, frozen

- ¼ teaspoon cinnamon

- 1 Apple

- Pinch of nutmeg

- 1 clove

- 3 ice cubes

Iceberg Peach Smoothie

- 1 cup Iceberg lettuce
- 1 Banana
- 1 peach
- 1 Brazil Nut
- 1 Mango
- 1 cup Kombucha (optional)
- Top with Hemp_seeds (optional)

Kiwi Apple & Leaf Lettuce Smoothie

- 1 cup Leaf Lettuce
- 2 Apples
- 2 kiwis
- 1/4 Lemon
- 1 tbsp. Chlorella (optional)
- 1 cup crushed ice

Banana Spinach Raspberry Smoothie

- 1 cup Spinach
- 2 Bananas
- 2 dates
- ½ cup Raspberries
- 1 tbsp. Ground flax seeds
- 1 cup crushed ice
- 1 tbsp. Cilantro

Endive Apples Smoothie

- 1 cup Endive
- 2 Apples
- 1 Tbsp. Dill
- 1 stalk Celery
- 1/2 Lemon
- 1 tbsp. Matcha (optional)
- 1 cup crushed ice

Spinach Celery Parsley Smoothie

- 1 cup Spinach

- 2 Peaches

- 1 avocado

- 2 stalks Celery

- 1 Lime

- 1 tbsp. Chia seeds

- 1 cup crushed ice

- 1 tbsp. Parsley

Cucumber Spinach Celery Carrot Smoothie

- 1 cup Spinach

- 2 Carrots

- 1 Cucumber

- 2 stalks Celery

- 1 Tbsp. Raw honey

- 1 tbsp. Parsley

- 1 cup crushed ice

Kale Cucumber Lime Apples Smoothie

- 1 cup Kale
- 2 Apples
- 1 avocado
- 1 Lime
- 1/4 cup Raspberries
- 1 Cucumber
- 1 cup crushed ice

Kiwi Zucchini Smoothie

- 1 cup zucchini

- 2 Apples

- 1/2 avocado

- 3 kiwis

- 1 tbsp. Spirulina (optional)

- 1 cup crushed ice

Avocado Kale Smoothie

- 1 cup Kale
- 1 Apple
- 2 avocados
- 1 stalk Celery
- 1/2 Lime
- 1 tbsp. Cilantro
- 1 cup crushed ice

Flax Kiwi Spinach Smoothie

- 1 cup Spinach

- 2 Apples

- 1 banana

- 1 stalk Celery

- 3 Kiwis

- 3 tbsp. ground <u>flax</u> seeds

- 1 cup crushed ice

Parsley Arugula Cucumber Apples Smoothie

- 1 cup Arugula
- 1 Cucumber
- 2 apples
- 1 stalk Celery
- 1 tbsp. Parsley
- 1 cup crushed ice

Celery Cucumber Cabbage Apples Smoothie

- 1/2 cup shredded cabbage

- 1 Apple

- 1 avocado

- 2 stalks Celery

- 1 Lemon

- 1 Zucchini

- 1 cup crushed ice

Kale Banana Apples Smoothie

- 1 cup Kale
- 2 Apples
- 3/4 avocado
- 1 banana
- 1 tbsp. Maqui (optional)
- 1 cup crushed ice

Zucchini Celery Apples Smoothie

- 1 zucchini
- 2 Apples
- 3/4 avocado
- 2 stalk Celery
- 1 jalapeno pepper
- 1 cup crushed ice

Leaf Lettuce Apples Spinach Smoothie

- 1/2 cup Spinach

- 2 Apples

- 2 Tbsp. almond butter

- 1 cup Leaf Lettuce

- 1/2 Lemon

- 1 tbsp. Chlorella (optional)

- 1 cup crushed ice

Zucchini Parsley Smoothie

- 1 zucchini

- 2 Apples

- ½ cup Parsley

- 1 stalk Celery

- ½ Lime

- 1 tbsp. Sesame seeds

- 1 cup crushed ice

Dandelion Banana Smoothie

- 1 cup Dandelion leaves
- 2 Bananas
- 3/4 avocado
- 1 Orange
- 1 tbsp. Spirulina (optional)
- 1 cup crushed ice

Leaf Lettuce Parsley Smoothie

- 1/2 cup Parsley

- 2 Apples

- 1 cup Leaf Lettuce

- 2 Tbsp. Sunflower butter

- 1 Yellow Grapefruit

- 1 tbsp. Hemp Hearts (optional)

- 1 cup crushed ice

Chia Apples Spinach Smoothie

- 1 cup Spinach
- 2 Apples
- 2 tbsp. Tahini
- 3 tbsp. Chia seeds
- 1 cup crushed ice

Grapefruit Kale Watercress Smoothie

- 1 large grapefruit
- 1 Apple
- 1 cup watercress
- 2 Kale leaves
- 1 Tbsp. dill (optional)
- 1 cup crushed ice

Collard Greens Parsley and Banana Smoothie

- 1 cup chopped collard greens

- 2 bananas

- 1 Tbsp. chopped parsley

- 1 tbsp. Chlorella (optional)

- 1 cup crushed ice

Dandelion Apples Smoothie

- 1 cup Dandelion leaves

- 1 orange

- 3/4 avocado

- 1 stalk Celery or 1 broccoli floret

- 1 tsp. chopped fresh ginger

- 1 cup crushed ice

Arugula Celery Apples Smoothie

- 1 cup Arugula or spinach

- 2 Apples

- 2 Tbsp. almond butter

- 1 tbsp. Chia seeds (optional)

- 1 cup crushed ice

Barley Grass Smoothie

- 1 cup barley grass or any other leafy greens

- 2 bananas

- 1 tbsp. chopped cilantro

- 1/4 lime

- 1 tsp. Spirulina (optional)

- 1 cup crushed ice

Yellow Smoothies

Cauliflower Smoothie

- 1 cup White cauliflower florets

- 1 Mango

- 1 passion fruit

- 1 tbsp. Bee Pollen (optional)

- 1 cup crushed ice

- Pinch of nutmeg

Mango Pineapple Smoothie

- 1 cup chopped Pineapple

- 1 Mango

- 1 cup Coconut Milk

- 1 tbsp. Goji berries (optional)

- 1 tbsp. of shredded coconut

Swiss Papaya Smoothie

- 1 Papaya
- 1 Banana
- 1 cup Swiss chard
- 1 cup Lemongrass tea
- 1 tbsp. Matcha (optional)

Apple Pineapple Smoothie

- 1 cup chopped Pineapple
- 1 Mango
- 2 Apples
- 1 banana
- 1 cup crushed ice
- 1 tbsp. Maca powder (optional)

Kiwi & Cauliflower Smoothie

- 1 cup White cauliflower florets
- 3 Kiwis
- 1 banana
- 1 tbsp. Bee Pollen (optional)
- 1 cup crushed ice
- Pinch of nutmeg

Cantaloupe Mango & Kiwi Smoothie

- 1 cup chopped Cantaloupe

- 1 Mango

- 3 kiwis

- 1 tbsp. Tahini

- 1 tbsp. Maqui (optional)

- 1 cup crushed ice

Banana & Mango Smoothie

- 2 bananas
- 1 Mango
- ½ lemon
- 1/2 tsp. Turmeric (optional)
- 1 cup crushed ice

Pineapple, Mango & Spinach Smoothie

- 1 cup Spinach

- 1 Mango

- 1 cup chopped pineapple

- 1 tbsp. Pumpkin seeds

- 1 cup crushed ice

- Pinch of nutmeg

Peach & Pineapple Smoothie

- 1 cup chopped peach

- 1 cup chopped pineapple

- 1 tbsp. ground flax seeds

- 1 cup crushed ice

- Pinch of cinnamon

- 1 tbsp. Almond butter

Maracuja Chia Mango Avocado Smoothie

- 1 cup chopped Maracuja (passion fruit)

- 1 Mango

- 2 tbsp. Chia seeds

- 1 cup crushed ice

- ½ Avocado

Ginger Mango Mint Yellow Pumpkin Smoothie

- 1 cup chopped Yellow Pumpkin

- 1 Mango

- 1 Yellow Grapefruit

- 1 tbsp. chopped Ginger

- 1 cup crushed ice

- 1 tbsp. Tahini

Orange & Mango Smoothie

- 1 cup chopped Mango
- 1 Orange
- 1 tbsp. Chlorella (optional)
- 1 cup crushed ice
- 1 tbsp. Sunflower butter
- Pinch of cinnamon

Avocado Mango Smoothie

- 1 Avocado
- 1 Mango
- 1 Grapefruit
- 1 tbsp. ground flax seeds
- 1 cup crushed ice

WHITE SMOOTHIES

Coconut Chia Pudding

- 1/4 cup Chia seeds

- 1 cup coconut milk

- 1/2 tablespoon Royall jelly

- 1 tsp. Ground Vanilla Bean

- a pinch of Nutmeg

- Top with Blueberries

White Kefir Smoothie

- ½ cup plain kefir

- 1 banana

- ¼ cup rolled oats

- 1 tablespoon sunflower butter

- 1 tbsp. Maca

- ½ tsp. Cinnamon

- Top with Apple slices, cherries and lime

Tzataziki Smoothie

- 1 cup kefir or plain Greek yogurt

- 1 cucumber

- 1 avocado

- 1 tbsp. Fresh dill or mint

- 1 tablespoon lemon juice

- 1 teaspoon sea salt

- 1 teaspoon Sesame seeds

Coconut Smoothie

- 1 cup of Coconut Milk

- 1 banana

- 2 White Peaches

- 1 tablespoon tahini

- 1 tbsp. Hemp seeds (optional)

- a pinch of Nutmeg

- Top with Coconut flakes

Cacao Blackberries Chia Pudding

- 1/4 cup Chia seeds

- 1 cup coconut milk

- 1/2 tablespoon Lucuma (optional, use raw honey instead)

- 1 tbsp. Maca (optional)

- Top with Blackberries

Coconut Yogurt Smoothie

- 1 Cup of low fat Greek Yogurt

- 1 banana

- 1 tablespoon Coconut flakes

- 1 tablespoon Hemp seeds (optional)

- Top with whipped Coconut Cream

Coconut Pomegranate Chia Pudding

- 1/4 cup Chia seeds

- 1 cup Coconut milk

- 1/2 tablespoon Raw honey

- 1/2 tablespoon Coconut flakes

- Top with Pomegranate seeds

Rainbow Smoothie

3 Colors Rainbow Smoothie

• Blend 1 Large beet with some crushed ice

• Blend 3 carrots with some crashed ice

• Blend 1 cucumber, 1 cup of leaf lettuce, some ice and ½ cup Wheatgrass

• Serve them separate to preserve the distinct color

RED SMOOTHIES

Carrot Date Smoothie

2 Carrots

2 Apples

1 cup of crushed ice

Pinch of nutmeg

½ tsp. Cinnamon

1 tbsp. Minced ginger

2 dates

Watermelon Apple smoothie

- 1 cup Seedless Watermelon
- ½ cup Pomegranate
- 2 apples
- 1/2 cup Raspberries
- 1 tbsp. Maqui (optional)
- 1 cup crushed ice

Watermelon Red Grapefruit Smoothie

- 1 cup seedless Watermelon

- 1 Red Grapefruit

- 1 cup spinach

- 1 cup crushed ice

- 2 tablespoons ground flax seeds

- 1 tbsp. Bee Pollen (optional)

Strawberry Carrot Smoothie

- 1 cup frozen strawberries

- 1 banana

- 1 carrot

- 1 cup crushed ice

- 2 tablespoons Hemp_seeds (optional)

- 1 tsp. Fresh Mint (optional)

Apricots & Carrots Smoothie

4 apricots

1 apple

1 cup spinach

2 carrots

1 cup crushed ice

1 tbsp. Maca (optional)

Strawberries Yogurt Smoothie

- 1 cup strawberries

- 1 cup low-fat plain yogurt

- 3 ice cubes

- 1 tbsp. Acai (optional)

Red Leaf Lettuce Smoothie

- 1/2 cup Lettuce
- 2 Bananas
- 1/2 Celery stalk (optional)
- 1/2 cup Strawberry
- 1/2 cup Raspberry
- 1 cup crushed ice
- 1 clove & pinch of nutmeg

Papaya Diva Smoothie

- 1 cup Endive
- 1 cup chopped Papaya
- 1 banana
- 1 tbsp. chopped fresh Ginger
- 1 cup crushed ice
- 1 tbsp. Cashew butter
- Top with Goji berries (optional)

Pomegranates & Berries smoothie

- 1 cup pitted Cherries

- ½ cup Raspberries

- 1 cup Pomegranates

- ½ cup Strawberries

- 1 cup Yerba Mate tea (optional, use any herbal tea instead)

- 1 tbsp. Chlorella (optional)

Avocado Carrot Smoothie

- 2 carrots

- 1 banana

- ½ avocado

- 2 apples

- Juice of ½ lemon

- 1 cup crushed ice

- 1 tsp. ginger

- Top with Bee Pollen (optional)

Red Currants Mellon Smoothie

- 1 cup melon

- 1 cup red currants (optional, use raspberries instead)

- 1 cup ginger tea

- 1 tbsp. raw honey

- 1 clove

- Pinch of nutmeg

- Pinch of cinnamon

- 1 tbsp. Chia Seeds (optional)

Blood Orange Smoothie

- 2 Blood Oranges

- 2 carrots

- 1 cup Raspberries

- 1 cup hibiscus tea

- 1 tbsp. Walnuts

- 2 tbsp. Ground flax seeds

Papaya Red Spinach Smoothie

- 1 cup chopped Papaya

- 1 banana

- 1 cup spinach

- 1 cup crushed ice

- 1 tablespoon Maca (optional)

- Top with 1 tablespoon dried chokecherries (optional)

Rainbow Smoothie

Green Layer: 2 Kiwis + 1/2 cup spinach + 2 ice cubes

Yellow Layer: 1 Mango + 1 Peach + 2 ice cubes

Red Layer: 1 cup of Strawberries + 1 cup of Raspberries

Frozen Berries Smoothie

1 cup frozen raspberries

1 cup frozen blueberries

1 cup of kefir

Pinch of nutmeg

1 tbsp. Minced ginger

Superfoods Smoothie Popsicles

Green Layer: 2 Kiwis + 1 Granny Smith apple + 1 ice cube

Yellow Layer: 1 Mango + 1 Orange + 1 ice cube

Red Layer: 1 cup of seedless watermelon + 1/2 cup of Raspberries

Pomegranate Watermelon Smoothie

1 cup seedless watermelon

1 cup Pomegranate seeds

1 cup of crushed ice

2 carrots

½ tsp. Mint

Orange Carrot Smoothie

2 Carrots

2 Oranges

1 cup of crushed ice

Pinch of cinnamon

1 tbsp. Minced ginger

1 tbsp. Chia seeds

Carrot Orange Papaya Smoothie

2 Carrots

1 Papaya

1 Orange

1 cup of crushed ice

Pinch of nutmeg

½ tsp. Cinnamon

1 tsp. Bee Pollen (optional)

Carrot Date Smoothie

2 Carrots

2 cups of chopped pumpkin

1 cup of crushed ice

Pinch of nutmeg

½ tsp. Cinnamon

1 tbsp. Minced parsley

1 tsp. pumpkin seeds

Pomegranate Yogurt Smoothie

1 cup Pomegranate seeds

2 ice cubes

1 cup of low fat yogurt

½ tsp. Bee Pollen (optional)

1 tbsp. sunflower seeds

Mango Papaya Mint Smoothie

1 chopped Mango

1 chopped Papaya

1 cup of crushed ice

Pinch of nutmeg

½ tsp. Mint

1 tbsp. Papaya Seeds

Papaya Carrot Pineapple Smoothie

2 Carrots

1 cup pineapple chunks

1 cup of crushed ice

1 cup chopped Papaya

½ tsp. Cinnamon

1 tbsp. Minced ginger

1 tbsp. Papaya seeds

Quatro Lamponi Mirtillo Negress Ribes Smoothie (4 Berries Smoothie)

½ cup raspberries

½ cup blueberries

½ cup blackberries

½ cup red currants

1 cup of crushed ice

Berries Kefir Smoothie

1/2 cup blackberries

½ cup raspberries

1/2 cup of crushed ice

1 cup Kefir

1 tbsp. Chia seeds

Red Currants Blueberry Smoothie

1 cup Spinach

1/2 cup blueberries

1/2 cup red currants

1 cup of crushed ice

Pinch of nutmeg

½ tsp. sesame seeds

Cucumber Carrot Date Smoothie

2 Carrots

2 Cucumbers

1/2 cup of crushed ice

½ tsp. Cinnamon

1 tbsp. Minced ginger

2 dates

Raspberry Sesame Smoothie

2 cups raspberries

2 Tbsp. tahini

1 cup of crushed ice

1 tbsp. Sesame seeds

Raspberry Cucumber Smoothie

1 cucumber

2 cups raspberries

1 cup of crushed ice

1 tbsp. Minced ginger

Blackberry Kefir Smoothie

1 cup Blackberries

1 cup Kefir

1 cup of crushed ice

½ tsp. mint leaves

2 lemon wedges for decoration

Cantaloupe Raspberry red Currant Smoothie

1 cup chopped cantaloupe

1 cup raspberries

1/2 red currants

1 cup of crushed ice

Pinch of nutmeg

Papaya Cauliflower Smoothie

1 chopped Papaya

1 cup cauliflower florets

1 cup of crushed ice

Pinch of nutmeg

1 Tbsp. Lucuma powder

1 tbsp. Minced ginger

Pumpkin Date Smoothie

2 Carrots

1 cup chopped pumpkin

1 cup of crushed ice

Pinch of nutmeg

½ tsp. Cinnamon

1 tbsp. Minced ginger

2 dates

Pumpkin Kefir Smoothie

1 cup chopped pumpkin

1 Apple

1 cup of crushed ice

Pinch of nutmeg

½ tsp. Cinnamon

Pumpkin smoothie top with Kefir and Pumpkin seeds

Cantaloupe Papaya Smoothie

1 chopped Papaya

1 cup chopped cantaloupe

1 banana

Juice from 1 lime

1 cup of crushed ice

1 tbsp. Minced ginger

PURPLE SMOOTHIES

Red Dragon Fruit (Pitaya) Smoothie

- 2 purple carrots

- 2 tbsp. Almond Butter

- 1 cup Red Dragon fruit (Pitaya)

- 1 tbsp. Maca (optional)

- 1 Blood Orange

- 1 cup crushed ice

Blueberry Yogurt & Chard Smoothie

- 1 cup blueberries

- 1 avocado

- 1 cup (Red) Chard

- 1 cup Yogurt

- 1/2 cup Mulberry (optional)

- 1 tbsp. Ground flax seeds

- ½ tsp. Cinnamon

- Top with Blueberries and Coconut flakes

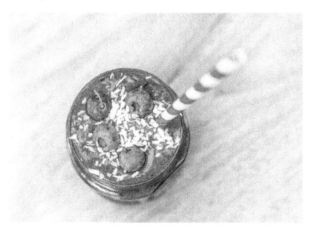

Beet Apple Smoothie

- 1 cup crushed ice

- 1/2 avocado, pitted

- 1 cup frozen strawberries

- 1 lemon, juiced

- 1 chopped celery stalks

- 1 large beet

- 1 apple

- 1 tablespoon coconut oil

- 1 tbsp. Acai (optional)

Blueberry Avocado Smoothie

- 1/2 avocado

- 1 cup spinach

- 1 cup blueberries, frozen

- 1 tsp. coconut oil

- 3/4 cup water

- 1 cup crushed ice

- Top with Cranberries

Purple Beet Smoothie

- 2 large beets
- ½ Avocado
- 1 cup Raspberry
- 1 tbsp. Chia seeds
- 1 carrot
- 1 cup crushed ice

Red Grapefruit & Beets Smoothie

- 1 Red Grapefruit

- 1 large beet

- 1/2 cup frozen sliced peaches

- 1/2 cup frozen strawberries

- 1/2 cup frozen mango chunks

- 1 tbsp. Maca (optional)

- 1 cup crushed ice

Blueberry Banana Smoothie

- 1 cup Blueberries

- 1 apple

- 1 banana

- 1 cup (Red) endive

- ½ cup crushed ice

- ½ cup water

- Top with Goji berries (optional) and shredded coconut

Purple Endive & Fig Smoothie

- 1 cup purple figs

- 1 banana

- 1 cup Endive

- 1 cup Raspberry leaf tea

- 1 tbsp Chia Seeds

- Top with chopped figs, 1 tbsp. Slivered Almonds and Blueberries

Purple Queen Smoothie

- 2 purple carrots
- 2 tbsp. Almond Butter
- 1 cup Red Dragon fruit (Pitaya)
- 1 tbsp. Maca (optional)
- 1 blood Orange
- 1 cup crushed ice

Black Smoothie

- 2 cups spinach
- 1 cup low fat plain yogurt
- 1 banana
- 1/2 cup blueberries, frozen
- 1 cup blackberries, frozen
- 1 tbsp. Cashew nuts
- 1 cup crushed ice

Blueberry Kefir & Spinach Smoothie

- 1 cup blueberries

- 1 cup chopped Cantaloupe

- 1 cup (Red) Spinach

- 1 cup Green tea

- 1 tbsp. Hemp_seeds (optional)

- ½ tsp. Cinnamon

Blackberry Yogurt & Purple Carrots Smoothie

- 1 cup blueberries

- 2 purple carrots

- 1 cup Yogurt

- 1 tbsp. ground flax seeds

- Top with Blackberries

Blackberry Banana Smoothie

- 1 cup blueberries

- 1 banana

- 1 cup of crushed ice

- ½ tsp. Cinnamon

- Top with Blackberries and Banana

Blueberry & Coconut Smoothie

- 1 cup blueberries
- 1 avocado
- 1 cup Coconut Milk
- 1banana
- ½ tsp. Cinnamon
- Top with Blueberries

Blueberry, Coconut Flakes & Sesame Seeds Smoothie

- 1 cup blueberries

- 1/2 cup shredded coconut flakes

- 1/2 cup Mulberry

- 1 tbsp. sesame seeds

- 1 cup of crushed ice

- a pinch of nutmeg

Blueberry & Kefir Smoothie

- 1 cup blueberries

- 1 cup Kefir

- 1/2 cup Raspberries

- ½ tsp. Spirulina (optional)

- Top with Blueberries and Mint leaves

Blueberry & Almond Smoothie

- 1 cup blueberries

- 1 banana

- 1 cup unsweetened Almond Milk

- 1 Tbsp. almond butter

- ½ tsp. Acai (optional)

- Top with Blueberries

Blueberry & Oatmeal Smoothie

- 1 cup blueberries

- 1 avocado

- 1/2 cup oats

- 2 bananas

- 1 cup of crushed ice

- ½ tsp. Chlorella (optional)

- Top with Blueberries and oatmeal flakes

Dragon Fruit & Banana Smoothie

- 1 cup chopped Dragon Fruit

- 1 avocado

- 1 banana

- 1 cup of crushed ice

- 1 tbsp. Chia seeds

Blueberry & Strawberry Smoothie

- 1 cup blueberries

- 1 cup Strawberries

- 1 banana

- 1 cup of crushed ice

- ½ tsp. Matcha (optional)

- Top with Blueberries

Blueberry, Kefir & Oats Smoothie

- 1 cup blueberries

- 1 cup oats

- 1 cup Kefir

- 1 tbsp. Ground flax seeds

Raspberry, Oats & Blueberry Smoothie

- 1 cup blueberries
- ¼ cup oats
- 1 cup raspberries
- 1 banana
- 1 cup of crushed ice
- 1 tsp. Maqui (optional)
- Top with Blueberries and oat flakes

Double Currants Smoothie

- 1 cup Black Currants

- 1 avocado

- 1 cup Red Currants

- 1 cup of crushed ice

- 1 banana

- 1 tbsp. Hemp Hearts (optional)

Blueberry & Dandelion Smoothie

- 1 cup blueberries
- 2 bananas
- 1 cup Dandelion
- 1 tbsp. Ground flax seeds
- 1 cup of crushed ice
- ½ tsp. Sesame seeds

Red Currants, Broccoli & Black Currants Smoothie

- 1 cup Black Currants

- ½ cup broccoli florets

- 1 cup Red Currants

- 1 avocado

- 1 cup of crushed ice

- 1 tsp. Spirulina (optional)

- ½ tsp. Cinnamon

Frozen Berries, Yogurt & Banana Smoothie

- 1 cup mixed frozen Berries
- 2 banana
- 1/2 cup Yogurt
- 1/4 cup Sunflower seeds
- 2 tbsp. Pumpkin seeds

Blueberry, Kefir, Coconut & Oats Smoothie

- 1 cup blueberries

- 1 avocado

- 1/2 cup oats

- 1 cup Kefir

- 1 tbsp. Ground Almond

- ½ tsp. shredded coconut

Blueberry Raspberry & Tahini Smoothie

- 1 cup blueberries
- ¼ tahini
- 1 cup Raspberries
- 1 tbsp. Ground flax seeds
- 1 cup of crushed ice
- Top with Blueberries flakes

Raspberry, Blueberry & Endive Smoothie

- 1 cup blueberries

- 1 avocado

- 1 cup Raspberries

- 1 cup of crushed ice

- 1/2 cup Endive leaves

- 1 banana

- ½ tsp. Cinnamon

- Top with Blueberries flakes

Banana, Chia & Blueberry Smoothie

- 1 cup blueberries

- 2 bananas

- 1 cup of crushed ice

- 1/2 cup Mulberry (optional)

- 2 tbsp. Chia seeds

- Top with Blueberries and Coconut flakes

Printed in Great Britain
by Amazon

27385488R00079

ISBN 9798853301771

9 798853 301771